Silent TEARS

Silent
TEARS

ADRENE M. WRIGHT

XULON PRESS

Xulon Press
2301 Lucien Way #415
Maitland, FL 32751
407.339.4217
www.xulonpress.com

Unless otherwise indicated, Scripture quotations taken from the King James
Version (KJV) – public domain

Scripture quotations taken from the New King James Version (NKJV).
Copyright © 1979, 1980, 1982 by Thomas Nelson, Inc. Used by permission.
All rights reserved.

Scripture quotations taken from the New Living Translation (NLT). Copyright
© 1996, 2004, 2007 by Tyndale House Foundation. Used by permission.
All rights reserved.

Scripture quotations taken from the HOLY BIBLE, New International Version
(NIV). Copyright © 1973, 1978, 1984, 2011 by Biblica, Inc.™. Used by
permission. All rights reserved.

Printed in the United States of America.

ISBN-13: 9781545605790

DEDICATION

This book is dedicated to the loving memory of my grandparents, Herbert and Louise Reaves, my aunt, Julia "Pie" Lee, and my father, Dandridge R. Allen. The four of you are undeniably entrenched in my heart and, without question, are four personal angels assigned to me. I will forever love you dearly.

To my children, DeMarco Mitchener and Chelsea Estes, your undying love, acceptance and support for your mother is a joy to my heart and a blessing to my soul. I'm so grateful to God for the bond we share, a cord tightly woven together that cannot be easily broken. In spite of all we've been through, you still have managed to develop your own relationship with Christ and have stood strong no matter the adversity that fell upon us. And, the beauty of it all, you've risen to the top. The greatest joy a mother could have is to know her children know God and are in relationship with Him for themselves. Thank you for sharing me with my Bible and my laptop! I love you with my everything!

TABLE OF CONTENTS

ACKNOWLEDGMENTS

I HAVE ALWAYS been taught to give honor where honor is due. So, without further ado, I could not go forward without acknowledging first Jesus Christ, my Lord and Savior. For without Him, none of this would be possible. Proverbs 3:6 states, "In all thy ways, acknowledge Him, and He shall direct thy paths." (KJV) For me, this scripture is so near and dear to my heart because it was He who directed me to pen this writing and I am quite confident that He will guide my path as a result of what is to come from its release.

There are so many that have supported and prayed for me as I began this process. I'll do my best not to forget anyone. However, if I do not mention your name, please charge it to my mind and not my heart. As a matter of fact, this book was prophesied three years prior to the actual writing. Pastor Christine Chandler, thank you for boldly speaking what the Lord had spoken to me privately. It was confirmation at the highest level and was clearly guided by the anointing of the Lord.

I praise God for my mother, Lucy Allen. Ma, ever since the day you gave birth to me, you have been there. For the most part, you shared the silent tears with me, not knowing what was wrong, but intuitively knowing something wasn't right. In your own way, you tried to solve every problem. However, there were many problems that only God could solve and/or needed to solve. Although I know it was hard for you to see me begin to depend more on Him than you, thank you for doing your best to understand, not giving up on me and knowing that I loved you no matter what. You truly are the epitome of "a mother's love".

To my sister, Twyle Pollard, we've come a long way and have been through so many things. But God...He has sustained us and knitted us together as only He can. Words cannot express my love and appreciation for you. Not only are you my sister, you are my friend and I'm so very proud of you. Thanks for going the extra mile, especially when it comes to Ma, so that I can peacefully fulfill the responsibilities of my calling and getting Wright One up and running. Thank you for your love, support, prayers and all those "gifts" that you gave when you knew I needed them the most. As Pie would say, "I have the best sister!"

To my niece, Kendra Pollard ("Go Aunts!"), my brother-in-law, Robert Pollard and my children DeMarco Mitchener and Chelsea Estes ("Ma, you got this!"), thank you for always being there. Your prayers, support and understanding during my high and low moments and the moments when I was locked in my room working, focused on trying to get this project, among many other projects, complete. Priceless.

To my aunt, Lillian Reaves, who instilled the gift of Administration in me from the time I was a child, approximately nine years old. Lillie, you have always taught me that I could accomplish anything that I put my mind to, with the help of the Lord. You taught me that it was possible to be beautiful inside and out, intelligent and God-fearing in one total package. Thank you for being a great example. You and Alisha (my "niece") Williams' prayers have not gone unnoticed... much love!

To my "sisters and BFFs" for over 30 plus years, Hope Harris and Christy L. Simmons, tears of joy when I think of you, your support, praise, sound wisdom and love shared. This project is as much yours, as mine because you two have prayed me through it all. Not once did you let the distance of two states, absent time, relationships or life's issues separate us. We always have the ability to pick up exactly where we left off, without missing a beat. Ladies, our connection is truly divine, anointed and appointed. I'm looking forward to the next 30 plus years.

To my Sisters With Purpose (SWP) Family! Too numerous to name all of you, but know that I love you with all my heart, mind and soul. I would not be here today without you and your love and prayers. Evangelist LaShaun Gabriel O'Bryant (and my O'Bryant and Gabriel Family) ...Lady, words cannot describe all that you mean to me. Thank you for being there and praying me through. To think, it all started with singing in Rejoice Choir together, some 20 years ago. We clearly didn't know what the Lord had in store for this divine connection. The evolution from sopranos to friends, to sisters, to partners in ministry has been nothing short of phenomenal.

The conversation on the bus trip to NY will never be forgotten! To Tiajuana Newton, Lisa Gillespie, Tonia Vines, Alva Catlett and Tonya Harrison – you all are a Board that is par none! SWP is so blessed to have such dedicated and committed leaders.

To my traveling sisters, Katrina Cherry, Jennifer Cherry, Debra Flowers, Gwendolyn James, Gwen Coleman, Marietta Newell and Wilma Hudson. Ladies, I adore you with my whole heart. So many laughs, so much fun. I'm so looking forward to the trips to come. Thanks for sound wisdom and praying me through.

To my "sisters", Valarie Barrett, Patricia Joyner, Kathy Driver, Jennifer Cherry, Gwen James, Tonia Vines, Paula Alston, Vanessa Armstrong, Zandra Nichols, Katrina Harling, Andrea Renfroe, Stephanie Williams, Lynn English, Frances Mack, Rev. Courtney Allen, Evangelist Glenda Smith and Michon Washington. You ladies have spoken into my life, seen me through and been there during those rough times, as well as the good. Priceless treasures you are.

To my taskmaster, Ernest Nelson, thank you for the constant prodding that ensured I stayed on track with my schedule and for the words of encouragement during those exhausting days. Your turn is next! Payback…LOL!

To my advisor and friend, Craig Edelin, thank you for the wisdom and guidance, especially during difficult times and during my time of transition. Your sound business acumen will never be forgotten. A priceless jewel, make no mistake, is what you are.

To the man of great stature, thank you for the wisdom, prayers and support. Seal Team 6 can't out do you! LOL! Much love!

To Dr. K. Jones, thank you. Not only were you a phenomenal employee, you were a great friend and counselor. The world has yet to discover the talent hidden within. As a dear friend and author would say, "It's time for you to Come Forth!"

To my nephew, Carrington Barbour, thank you. You are a man who's wise beyond his years, with a discerning spirit beyond compare. Thank you for wisdom, prayers and support and, particularly, for the talks and laughter that helped me get on the other side of "thru". I'm so very proud of you. Much love!

To Clifton and Frances Mitchener, Joanne Estes and Betty Smith, thank you. I praise God for the bond of love we share. Agape love at its finest!

Thank you to those who shared personal experiences with me on this journey called life. Thank you, for the various situations we endured resulting in personal growth and a closer walk with God. You know who you are…

To Pastor Linwood Grant, these last six years being under your guidance and direction have been extraordinary. I have learned SO much from you. Not only do you love God with your everything, it's reflected in your everyday actions. You exemplify exactly what the Bible teaches…love in action. Not only have I grown as a Minister, I've grown as a person, which has caused me to be better for all those connected to me. Thank you for helping me to perfect the gifts given unto me by God and for boldly proclaiming what "thus saith the Lord"!

To First Lady Jackie Grant, the Ministerial Staff and Min. Michael Woolard, the Deacons/ Deaconesses, the Trustees, the Mothers' Ministry, the Women's Ministry of St. Judah, the Administration Department and the entire St. Judah Family, words cannot express what you mean to me. St. Judah, we are blessed to have the best Pastor on this side of Jordan and I'm blessed to have you as my Church

Family. Thank you for believing God in the things concerning me. Unending love for you!

Pastor Lisa Gillespie, I just don't know where to begin. You believed God for what He told you concerning me 10 years ago, and you are still believing Him today on my behalf. I praise God for all that you've poured into my life and that of my children. Thank you and my "niece" Markisha Barber, for all the prayers and support. Lisa, words cannot express what your assistance on completing this project means to me. You have been a friend, a sister, a mentor and a confidante. From the beginning of the blank page, until the last period, you were there... unforgettable!

Last, but certainly not least, to Don Newman, Michelle Gil and the Xulon Press Family...thank you. Don and Michelle, I will never forget our very first meeting and how the anointing of the Lord was so powerful on that beautiful day in January. The words spoken that day have been embedded in me and will never be forgotten. Thank you for believing what God showed you concerning *Silent Tears* before the book was completed. To God be the glory!

INTRODUCTION

TEARS, AS DESIGNED by God, are a natural lubricant for our eyes to keep them moistened and prevent them from drying out. Tears are also used to help keep foreign particles out of our eyes, as defined by Google. Tears generate a saline fluid, which I believe is God's mechanism for cleansing, as saline (salt) is often used as a cleansing or healing agent. When tears flow down due to emotions we are experiencing, it's the body's way of cleaning out impurities held within the soul. When we withhold our tears and refuse to cry, we are going against the natural process created by God to remove foreign particles or toxins from within. These toxins can bring on a myriad of negative emotions, stress and subsequent illnesses (i.e. cancer, heart disease, kidney disease, etc.) and possibly death because of our refusal to release that which has caused us angst.

Sadly, society has taught us that crying is a sign of weakness, particularly for a man. And, in these days and times, it's not appropriate for a woman to cry either, especially in the workplace, because she is then seen as weak and emotional. However, holding onto negative emotions and thoughts and the refusal to address painful situations is not a sign of strength. It's really a sign of weakness and exhibits the spirit of pride and the spirit of control, which is a form of witchcraft. Granted, I'm not suggesting that you walk around blubbering all the time for there is a time and a place for everything. What I am suggesting that you do is to address your situation with the One who has the ability to help you resolve it. For when we hold onto that which is toxic, we are saying to God that we know better than He does on how to deal with our hurtful situations. We are being disobedient to His Word which tells us to cast our cares upon Him. What we don't realize is that we are also operating under the manipulation of the enemy. It's a trick!

Through my years of silent tears, I have seen within myself and others how unresolved issues and feelings can cause one to become a big ball of anger – a ticking time bomb, if you will. Ultimately, the person ends up masking their pain through methods of temporary relief such as substance abuse or addictions to vices such as overeating, shopping or sexual promiscuity. The feelings and emotions may also surface through unexplained illnesses or anger management issues. One may say the aforementioned seems to be extreme or way out in left field but the reality is that unre-solved issues grow and spread like uncontrollable weeds in a garden. Eventually, the beauty of the garden, if not properly tended, will be overtaken by the weeds, choking the life out of what was once beautiful. So it is with unresolved issues; they will kill your soul.

As you travel through *Silent Tears*, you will embark upon a journey visiting situations that I've encountered over the years that caused me to cry silently. For, you see, on the outside, I was smiling and going ahead as if all were well. Yet, on the inside, there were times when I felt as if I was going to die...or simply just wanted to die. If it had not been for my relationship with Jesus Christ, my Lord and Savior, and the prayers of very dear family members, friends and spirtual mentors, I would have catapulted into an abyss from which I'm not so certain I would have returned. But God…

Silent Tears discusses various life issues for which we find ourselves crying silently. Areas such as bad choices, love, tragedy, death, persecution and financial matters, just to name a few. The topics discussed herein are not all inclusive, but rather a sprinkling of a few. The desire is that by the end of reading this book, you will find hope and allow the Lord to restore an inner peace and joy within you that only He can provide. For our "…hope is built on nothing less than Jesus' blood and righteousness…" (My Hope Is Built On Nothing Less)[1]

At the end of each chapter, you will find space for your own personal reflections.
After reading this book, I pray that you will allow yourself to cry and your soul to heal.
Prayer:

> *Father, I come in the name of thy son, Jesus, lifting up the person reading this book right now. Lord, I ask that you decrease them and increase You in them as they begin to journey through the pages of this book. As they begin to*

reflect on circumstances in their life, revisiting situations of their own past, may they allow you to process them through to the very end. I bind, in the name of Jesus, any spiritual forces of darkness that will try to hinder them from completing this reading and/or causing them to be overcome with doubt, guilt, shame, anger, bitterness or frustration. May they not be tormented in situations revealed from their past. Let Your glory be revealed and the healing begin. Let them receive what thus sayeth the Lord. May this book not be seen as entertainment but as a tool to enable them to overcome the obstacles that cause them their own silent tears. It's in Your name Jesus that I pray...Amen!

To God be the glory!

Chapter 1

CHOICES

"The thief cometh not, but for to steal, and to kill, and to destroy: I am come that they might have life, and that they might have it more abundantly." John 10:10 KJV

SURBURBAN LIVING – a lifestyle that causes you to be close enough to the city to enjoy its essence, its excitement and its culture. Yet, far enough away to allow you to venture from chaos to calm, to live peacefully while feeling safe, protected and secure. For some surburbanites, you couldn't pay them any amount of money to go into the city for any reason. It's a choice.

Some choose to live in the city, embracing all that it has to offer. To them, the city represents energy and vitality. They feel that living in the suburbs means life is over and the excitement has gone. Others prefer the calm of the suburbs, feeling the city will expose them to way more than they bargained for. It's a choice.

Then, there are those who are right on the line. The benefit of this is that it allows easy access to city life, while at the same time, providing the benefits of the suburbs, one of which is lower property taxes. For lack of better words, they straddle.

Isn't it interesting that our natural state of livimg is a reflection of our spiritual state of living? Again, it's a choice. Some see the city as worldly living and some see the suburbs as Christian living. For some reason, there is a misperception that being a Christian is dull. Because of that line of thinking, many straddle the fence. They straddle because they fear that if they totally commit to Christ, they will miss out on life. It makes one wonder, what are they really missing?

The Learner's Dictionary defines choice as "the act of picking or deciding two or more possibilities. It's the opportunity or power to make a decision: a range of things that can be chosen".[2] As a child of the most High God, we also learn through reading the Bible that God gives us a choice. He calls it "free will". We learn that living the life of a Christian is not a dictatorship; but, an opportunity to make choices. In other words, God gives us power or authority to make a decision. As a matter of fact, there is an old adage that says the Bible is our "**B**asic **I**nstructions **B**efore **L**eaving **E**arth". With that said, it's easy to infer that God provides the instructions for us to live by, but the choice to follow those instructions is up to us. So, how, as believers in Christ, can we really get upset with God for our position in life when the decisions we have made were entirely left up to us?!!

You know, when I finally accepted the assign-ment from God to write this book, in my mind, "**I**" had decided that it would not be autobiographical in nature. But clearly, one can see that it was <u>my deci-sion</u> and not the Lord's. However, in being realistic and in understanding that my life is not my own and, certainly this assignment is not my own but God's, my personal experiences will seep through and be entwined throughout. For how can I effec-tively minister unto you if I don't share what God has brought me through in an effort to help you? To be an effective witness, I must speak truth based on God's Word and not of my own personal opinion.

Rest assured, if our paths have crossed, your part in any of my ups and downs will not be exposed!

Another reason that personal experiences may be expounded upon is so that I can help others grow as God has shown me. The Lord is an amazing and awesome wonder! Too often, we take for granted the experiences we have had or the positions He has placed us in; we do not recognize them as jewels. We often become upset because we are not where we want to be or where we are supposed to be. Life's issues and challenges come before us when what we really want is smooth sailing. We don't want to deal with anything, not realizing and recognizing that the Potter (God) takes us (the clay) back to mold us on the Potter's wheel and to perfect that which has become imperfect. He wants to fix those cracks, expose and seal those leaks that would otherwise afford the opportunity for the unholy to saturate our being, which is His artwork. He wants to be able to reshape us into who He has called us to be. As a quote from my son, paraphrasing of course, "sometimes it takes for us to go back to the furnace, not for our purpose, but to show others who He is to us." Yes, sometimes, we have to go through things to deliver us, heal us, clean us up or whatever the case may be. But sometimes, we simply go through things so others can see that God is real, He's within us, He's walking with us and that He has us in the palm of His hand. No matter the reason that we go through our challenges, the ultimate result should be that God gets the glory.

I praise God for all things and for enduring all situations. No, life is not always easy and quite frankly, difficulties are not always a result of something somebody has done to us. Often they are as a result of the choices we make. Decisions to forego, decisions to procrastinate, decisions of not trusting or not believing. No matter our rationale, our choices are <u>our choices</u>. Some of the choices have been good; some not so good. Some choices were based on God's Word; some based on simply doing what we wanted to do. Whether it was out of stubborness, rebellion or wanting what we wanted when we wanted it, we made the choice.

There have been times when God may have spoken about obtaining some things or achieving some things or reaching some goals. However, even in our revelations from God, we have a choice. The accurate decision would be to move as directed by Him, so as not to miss His timing. We have to always remain prayerful and vigilant in moving in the precise moment directed by Him. If God has given you a vision, it will come to pass. We have to consciously choose not to jump before God's timing. To do so could cause us to miss out and mess up; ultimately placing us in situations that are not of Him and certainly not His best for us.

So, as you read though this book, try to soak up what the Lord is saying. Ask Him to decrease you and increase Him in you so that you may receive what He's relaying to you for this season. There are some things that He's trying to help you with, deliver you from, or prevent you from embarking upon. God has a way of giving us warning signals. His Spirit speaks to us. But, we need to do a better job of listening to Him. And, I say "we" because we all are remiss at times. By paying attention, we will come to understand Romans 8:28 (NKJV), *"… all things work together for the good to those who love God, to those who are called according to His purpose."* All things means that some things will be good, some things will not be so good; however, collectively, when gathered together, all will be well. God makes no mistakes. He didn't when He created us. So, it certainly isn't in the plans and purpose He has for our lives. Jeremiah 29:11 (KJV) tells us that *"He knows the purpose and plans He has for our lives; not to harm us, but to give us a future and a hope."*

Will you trust Him? Trust Him as you read? Trust Him as He takes you on a journey, in His infinite wisdom, to give you all He has for you? Habakkuk 2:2-3 (NKJV) says, *"Record the vision and make it plain on tablets, so that he may run who reads it. For the vision is yet for the appointed time; but at the end it will speak and it will not lie. Though it tarries, wait for it; because it will surely come, it will not tarry."* We see the vision but we stumble during the process. Getting to where God will have us to go is a process. And, in the midst of the process, there are some things He will need to break off, to prune, to burn off us as He molds us again afresh and anew. This is so that we don't lose what we obtain and so that we can handle the place to which He is taking us. It's also to teach others and show the love of God and be able to speak of His goodness. He's giving us an opportunity to share the Kingdom of God with others. And, with the success He blesses us with, we can pour back into the Kingdom. It's not for us to hoard for ourselves. It's not for us to say, "I got mine, now you get yours." It's for us to reach back, to give back, to show others the way so that we can see Jesus and hear Him say, "...*well done, thou good and faithful servant.*"(Matthew 25:21 KJV)

Choices. Your first choice begins right now. You can continue in the journey on how to walk out the Word of God in your life. Or, you can put the book down and continue life status quo. What is your choice?

REFLECTIONS

_____

_____

_____

_____

_____

_____

_____

_____

_____

_____

_____

_____

_____

_____

_____

_____

Chapter 2

THE BEGINNING

"I knew you before I formed you in your moth-er's womb. Before you were born I set you apart and appointed you as a prophet to the nations."
Jeremiah 1:5 NLT

THERE IS AN old saying that states, "If I knew then, what I know now, I'd be in a different place." Well, for me, there's some truth to that statement. You see, my journey with knowing who God is began as a child. I found out later, as I matured, that knowing who He is and being in relationship with Him are two very different things. I know who the President is but I'm not in relationship with him. He's not a part of my "inner circle." However, God IS my circle, my core. He's a core that defines the very essence of who I am.

For many years, I struggled with life's issues and choices I made because I was not walking as the daughter of <u>the </u>King. I was not walking in the boldness of God. Oh, I was bold alright; I was rough around the edges for sure. One of my best friends from high school said I was a bully. Of course, I didn't think so then nor do I think so now. At least, not in the context for which the statement was made. If I were to be called a bully today, I'd proudly say that I am – I'm a bully for Jesus, that is! But, what I've always been is bold, outspoken and not afraid of too many people. I was raised on the principle that I put my pants on one leg at a time, like every other person. Therefore, no one was better than me...just different. And, we were taught to respect each other's differences. I was also raised under parents and grandparents who held high standards and who were disciplinarians. However, the spirit of control also existed and was a generational curse. I just didn't recognize it until I was in my 30s and, by then, there was much work for God to do.

I have no complaints about my upbringing, for it taught me how to be strong, how to endure and how to trust in the Lord. The parental rules were strongly enforced, kept me out of trouble and from traveling down a path that could have been far worse. It's interesting that today, what some call control was simply good old-fashioned discipline. I cringe that the difference has not been defined, but instead more often dismissed. I don't regret the discipline because it was necessary. A controlling spirit is one that prides itself on exercising dominance or influence over another to direct a person's behavior or control the course of events. It is manipulation in its purest sense. Discipline, however, is the act of training people to obey rules or a code of behavior, using punishment to correct obedience (Oxford Dictionary).[3]

My grandmother was a strong proponent of Proverbs 22:6, which says, *"Train up a child in the way he should go. And, when he is old, he will not depart from it."* We were always taught to "trust in the Lord". But, growing up, we really did not understand what it meant to trust in the Lord. As children, teenagers and young adults, we just knew we needed to do our best to stay out of trouble, avoid bringing shame to the family name and "thank God" for all those times that we didn't get caught doing what we should not have been doing. We didn't really comprehend the depth of what it meant for God to have us in the palm of His hand or to understand the number of people who were praying for us. The reality of our relationship with God and coming into the full knowledge of who He is did not occur until we were "grown" and out on our own, facing life's challenges. It was then that we began to realize that we were in dire need of a Savior. But even then, unless under the right spiritual guidance and teaching, many of us tend to give our lives to Christ and then leave Him right at the altar where we met Him. Unfortunately, those who are not under the right teaching are not taught how to deal with life's issues as a Christian once they get up from their knees. It is imperative that Ministers of the Gospel teach Believers how to apply and "walk out" God's Word in their daily lives.

How does one "walk out" the Word of God? Where is God during the midst of life's storms? So many times, you hear the anguish in the voices of others or even within yourself, as you cry out:

❖ Lord, Your Word teaches me that you'll never leave me or forsake me, so how come I feel so alone?

❖ Where were you God, when my mother, father, spouse, sibling, or child died? Where were you God when I lost my job, had no food on the table, lost my house, car, land?

❖ Where were you God, when I had nowhere to turn?

❖ Why wouldn't you just let me take my life?

❖ Why am I going through a bitter divorce? You said we'd be together until death do us part.

❖ Why is my spouse or child in prison? Strung out on drugs and/or alcohol? Selling her body as a prostitute?

❖ Where is my "happily ever after"?

This is just a small sampling of questions that have been asked of God by His children. Questions that have caused some to cry openly, but more often, to cry silently. After all, many Christians are "blessed and highly favored, fire-baptized and living for the Lord!" How could they possibly go through such anguish? And, realistically speaking, hearing the words "that which tries us, makes us stronger" does not easily soothe our pain when we are "going through". As a matter of fact, the Bible teaches us that there will be times when we must encourage ourselves.

King David, through the Book of Psalms, is a great guide in teaching us how to encourage ourselves. David, although a man who fell many times, was known to be loved by God because he had a heart for God. Which means that, no matter what he went through, he was not afraid to go to God, whether it be in praise or in confession. He did not cover up or deny his many sins and shortcomings, his mistakes or his pain. David made sure that he blessed the Lord at all times during the good and the bad. As a matter of fact, it's through David that we learn about prayer and praise. Psalm 138:3 (KJV) says, "*As soon as I pray, you answer me; you encourage me by giving me strength*". When we cry out to God in supplication, pouring our entire being into conversing with Him, He hears us, will answer us and encourage us on how to move forward. But, we HAVE to talk to Him. Psalm 31:22 (KJV) tells us that "*God hears our cry for mercy and answers our call for help.*"

REFLECTIONS

_____

_____

_____

_____

_____

_____

_____

_____

_____

_____

_____

_____

_____

_____

_____

_____

Chapter 3

TEARS OF LOVE LOST

"This is my commandment: Love each other in the same way I have loved you. There is no greater love than to lay down one's life for one's friend. You are my friend if you do what I command." John 15:12-14 NLT

LOVE, A SMALL but powerful word. A word that is spoken in so many ways...in honesty, in deceit, in joy and in pain. Love, a word that brings so much happiness and equally as much sadness when gone wrong. Love, a word that is used as a disguise to obtain that which the speaker does not deserve. When misused, it often hurts to the core. However, when understood as it was intended by God, who is Love, then it can be a beautiful thing.

Growing up was very interesting for me. I was overweight and often told that I had a "cute face".

However, although overweight and "smart", I never really had a problem with being liked by boys. My grandmother had taught me at a very early age the key to being confident, even though I was bigger than other girls in my class. Her words have stuck with me all my life, even as I traveled the "yo-yo" of managing my weight. She taught me to make sure my clothes were neat and pressed, clean and proportionate to my size. In other words, don't wear anything too tight or too revealing that would expose my "assets". I was taught to give a boy/man "something to think about" because if you show everything, then there is nothing for him to look forward to. Grandma made sure I was equipped in the finer principles of womanhood as it related to demeanor, cleanliness, jewelry, clothing, perfume, shoes and handbags. I also cannot forget the art of cooking and keeping a clean home. My grandmother was always well-dressed, dignified and full of grace.

However, Grandma wasn't the only one. I liken myself to being a unique blend...a city girl with a country twang. Between my mom, my sister, aunts, female cousins and some really, really good girl-friends, over time I learned how to be confident in who I am and what I bring to the table...not in an arrogant or conceited way, but in a self-respectful way. You see, I was taught to love myself, just because of the mere fact that God loved me first. And even after enduring many hurtful situations at the hands of men, it was my grandfather, father, my Pastors and the teachings of Bishop T.D. Jakes "Woman Thou Are Loosed" book[4], Bible[5] and series,[6] that taught me that my greatest love came from God. I learned that I was fearfully and wonderfully made, was chosen and a "designer original". As Bishop Jakes stated in his "Pearls" section from his *Woman Thou Are Loosed* Bible[7], I was "haute couture fashion" in the eyes of God.

However, back to Grandma; she was also a strong woman. "Foolishness" was not to be tolerated from anyone. She was very straightforward, so you always knew where you stood. Although Grandma didn't always say the words, "I love you", she showed you through her words of praise about you to others and the little things she did, such as fixing your favorite dish or her smile that lit up the room when you walked through the door. Her face revealed her feelings, so you knew when you made her proud and when you didn't.

As I'm sure you have figured out by now, she was a great influence in my life; although, in my younger years, I must admit that I didn't think she loved me because I was always being compared to one of my cousins. It was as if I wasn't good enough because I didn't act the same as she. Let's just say that my cousin spent more time in church than I did and was more reserved and demure than I. For you see, while growing up, my parents were neither regular churchgoers or demure. They were workaholics and displayed their love for me in a different manner through material gifts. The seeds, as it relates to the things of God, were planted by my grandmother and watered by my aunts. I spent many summers and school breaks with them and they made sure I grew up "in the Lord". As I grew older and closer in my relationship with the Lord, I realized the depth of the love that Grandma had for all her children, and, yes, she really did love me.

Like most women, I've been through some good relationships and some not so good relationships. I've loved and I've lost. I've been date-raped and have been loved with much passion and abandon. I've lived with having to deal with an extra-marital affair which resulted in the other woman becoming pregnant, my spouse's addiction to crack cocaine and run-ins with the law and then a spouse's verbal and mental abuse of me and my children. Being a woman who expected "happily ever after" in marriage, with the house, picket fence and two children, engaging in multiple marriages was its own pain in and of itself. Certainly, nothing I am proud of, intended or wanted to do. Needless to say, in my mind and from a place of hurt, I've been saying to myself "never again". Yet, I quietly hear the Lord saying, "Did I say that?" Whatever the future, just the thought brings about silent tears. For, I know that in spite of it all, God will use the events that He brought me through to help someone else along the way.

But the tears didn't stop there. I believe the cruelest twist of fate is the agony of lost love because of wrong timing. There is nothing worse than the resurfacing of your high school sweetheart, amid devastating times, and having to walk away. In addition, the realization that the person was "the one who got away". Yet, you still have to trust that God knew best and accept that it just may not have been meant to be. There is an old saying that "the heart wants what the heart wants" and when your heart's desires are lined up with the Will of God for your life, that's certainly true. However, the struggle comes when the heart yearns for that to which it has no access or rights. That's where integrity comes in and faith and trust in God must take a stand. It also helps too that the other party is of great stature inside and out; ensuring that integrity for all is preserved. And when you both put your faith and trust in God, you find that He can preserve the love and friendship without com-promise to who He's called you to be.

Last, but certainly not least, there are the silent tears from having to walk alone. The tears that come from a person who wants to be in a loving relationship, yet is on the path of walking alone. The tears and agony of going to "couples" events solo, while your husband opts to either work or run the streets rather than escort you. The tears of being a romantic, yet not having anyone to do "romantic" things with, such as the honeymoon of your choice, anniversary celebrations, trips to the Caribbean, resorts solely for couples, marriage retreats, etc. And although, the goodness, strength and peace of the Lord will not allow you to miss out on the joy of participating in as many of these things that can also be done alone or with friends, it still doesn't mean there will not be that initial sting. I just praise God that He's surrounded me with a wonderful support system of family and friends who bring laughter and joy into my life so that the sting is very, very brief and less painful as time goes by. I'm grateful.

Through it all, I survived. I have shed many a tear because I have yet to receive my "happily ever after". Tears that I've hidden from family and friends because of wearing the mask of one who is "blessed and highly favored". Silently crying within because I didn't feel blessed by God nor highly favored when it came to love and having a lasting marriage. Experiencing the agony of "What did I do wrong?" or "What could I have done better?", until ultimately coming to the realization that some things just weren't meant to be. It was also realizing that Romans 8:28 (KJV) is true in that *"And we know all things work together for the good to them that love God, to them who are called according to His purpose"*, the person that He has for me has to be strong and able to handle the path that God has orchestrated. For, this is a journey that we will walk together, with my "Boaz" taking the lead. For Amos 3:3 (KJV) states, *"Can two walk together, except they be agreed?"*

Most importantly, I had to learn that the "Boaz", as described in the Book of Ruth, that I so desperately desired, I already had. My Kinsman-Redeemer is Jesus. No one can take care of me like He can. And, quite frankly, whoever is for me, must love Him more than he loves me. Because if He can't and doesn't love the Lord with his whole heart, he surely will not know how to love me as Jesus loves the Church. And, we both must understand that we are gifts given to each other by God, connected for divine purpose.

REFLECTIONS

Chapter 4

TEARS OF HEART-WRENCHING PAIN

"Yea, though I walk through the valley of the shadow of death, I will fear no evil: For thou art with me, thy rod and thy staff they comfort me."
Psalm 23:4, KJV

ONE OF THE worst pains that a parent can experience is the death of their child. After all, the child is supposed to bury their parent, not the other way around. However, there is a pain that is just as agonizing. It's the pain of coming within a few hours of losing your child and then standing by silently as the hospital team works feverishly to save her life. On the outside, you are doing your best effort to keep a brave, confident face for your child. Trying desperately not to show the gamut of emotions that are raging on the inside; doing your absolute best to hold the floodgate of tears from streaming down your face. All the while, on the inside, you are silently screaming a guttural, "NO, God! NOOOOO!!!" at the top of your lungs. It's the pain of telling your child everything is going to be okay, when in fact you really don't know because of the thousands of questions you, yourself, have as the doctors work to pinpoint the root cause of the illness.

This heart-wrenching pain is the anguish of finally learning that your child has a disease that is life threatening and not knowing where, how or when it all came about. Was it something in your genes or the genes of her father? Is it a generational curse? It's the pain of an extremely urgent rush to get the fluid off her heart and lungs before she expires right in your presence. A procedure that is so critical to her life that it's done in the room, as opposed to going into an operating room. It's hearing the doctor tell you your child has END STAGE renal disease. END STAGE? That means no hope, right? Wrong! What do you mean, doctor, that the only way my child will survive is being hooked up to a dialysis machine three times a week until or if and when she gets a transplant? Wrong!

She WILL get a kidney and won't be hooked up to a machine for the rest of her life!!!

It's the silent tears of walking the corridor of the hospital's intensive care unit and seeing children with tubes sticking out of all parts of their bodies, while the parents are nestled closely by, in anguish, shock and/or disbelief. It's the silent tears of watching hospital staff rush down the hall with crash carts with mixed emotions – praying it's not your child's room and joyful on the inside when it isn't; yet, hurting for the family whose child is the recipient of the emergency care. It's the silent tears of praying for the family whose child didn't make and enduring the blood curdling wail of pain and sorrow, while your stomach is in knots.

But, I believe the most agonizing part of the whole process for me was waiting for the Word that the Lord had given me to come to pass. I clearly remember asking God why this happened to my baby. What had I done wrong to elicit such trauma for her? Should I just walk totally on faith and forego dialysis for her altogether? After all, at the time, she was only thirteen and the responsibility for the decision rested upon me. Was my faith strong enough for the both of us? Lord, what would You have me to do?

Immediately, I went into prayer and petitioned God from a place that I didn't even know existed. It's funny how we can think we are strong in faith and trust in God until life hits us right square between the eyes, only to find out our faith level still has room to grow. But then again, faith is like a mustard seed and, as with all properly watered seeds, it's expected to grow. I heard the Lord clearly state that my daughter's condition was temporary. I was instructed to share that she was not "sick" but that she had a "condition", which had a "coming in and a going out". It was a posture that my children and I hold onto even until this day. He also stated that this situation was not necessarily for her, but for someone else. For, you see, the success of our getting on the other side of "through" is dependent solely upon our response to the issue at hand. When things go wrong in our lives, we can have a negative response with little or no faith and trust or we can have a positive response and a willingness to stretch our faith and trust in Him.

<u>Now</u>, I more clearly understand why the Lord tells us that we must hide His Word within our heart. For it is during trying times, when you may not have a Bible at your immediate disposal, that you must pull from what you have within. And, as you go through the process, pulling from within can be agonizing for tests will come. For me, my marriage was tested. The countless hours at the hospital during her initial three weeks in the hospital; days, weeks and months of dialysis, and then finally the receipt of a kidney, resulting in additional weeks in the hospital. What didn't help is that the support wasn't there from the one I felt I needed the most and I felt all alone. I praise God for my son, my family and friends and the numerous people across the nation who prayed for us during this journey of almost two years. You see, temporary wasn't a few weeks or months, as I initially expected. It was twenty-one very long months. There would be days where I would be totally exhausted. I was working by day, spending at least four hours at the hospital and then going back to work and it was exhausting. Then, couple that with school (I was pursuing and obtained my Bachelors) and responsibilities that I

had as a Minister of the Gospel. There were times that I didn't even know my name. Instead of compassion, most days I received anger and attitude from my husband. Looking back, I'm sure that he probably felt that there was no room for him. That was a trick of the enemy and it worked. For had we shared the load, as husband and wife should, we would be in a different place today. Yet, I've learned that which tries you makes you stronger and it's through adversity that true character traits are revealed.

I'm so grateful that I can say the joy of the Lord is my strength. I learned that my children and I were built for this and we have quite the testimony to what God can do when you believe. He most definitely is the Ultimate Healer and Restorer of our soul! But to be so, we had to believe, had to diligently seek Him through His Word and continuously praise Him, even during the darkest hours.

REFLECTIONS

_____

_____

_____

_____

_____

_____

_____

_____

_____

_____

_____

_____

_____

_____

_____

_____

Chapter 5

TEARS DUE TO THE LOSS OF LOVED ONES

"Don't let your heart be troubled. Trust in God, and trust also in me." John 14:1

DEATH. A WORD that can cause one to cringe at the very sound, mention or notification of it. Even when we know that the death of a loved one is pending, notification of its actual occurrence can still throw us into a tailspin. And, when we hear of unexpected death, for many, that's another ballgame altogether. Even to Believers who understand that *"to be absent from the body is to be present with the Lord"* (2 Corinthians 5:8), the sting of death can momentarily shake us. The reality is that we would love to have our loved ones with us for a lifetime. No one wants to see someone that's near and dear to them die, even when knowing they are "in a better place" or "free from pain". What doesn't help is the adage of "death comes in threes", meaning that there will be three deaths of people you know over a short period. Tears…

A very dear sister-friend of mine, who is one of my best friends and mentors and a dynamic minister of the Gospel was preaching the eulogy of a family member. During the service, she posed a very poignant question… "Is there really a good time to die?" When you think about it, that's a very thought provoking question. When it's your time of transition, it's not like you can ask the Lord to come back later when your calendar is free because at that moment you have an appointment or a matter to which you must attend. Coming back "next Thursday at 2 p.m." is not an option. The number of people who are prepared and ready to go home to be with the Lord, having "their affairs in order" and having made peace with those connected to them is grossly outweighed by the ones who are not prepared. Even those who are terminally ill may struggle during the last days of their lives, presumably recapping the ups and downs, mistakes, choices, regrets, joys, pains, etc. In other words, their lives are replayed before their very eyes. They may try to get as much of their "to do list" or their "bucket list" completed as possible. But, oftentimes, there are still one, two or more things they leave undone.

In reality, sadness and questions are felt by the loved ones who are left behind. Losing a loved one is not easy to accept, let alone comprehend. Even when a loved one leaves "too soon", no matter how strong your relationship is with the Lord, grappling with the fact that it was "in His timing" is hard to fathom. It's ironic that we can accept that God chose us and knew when we were going to be born and when we were going to die and that "…*there is a time and a season for everything under the sun…*" (Ecclesiastes 3) until it comes to the death of a loved one. Tears will flow, either publicly or privately. The real key is to ensure that the silent tears don't flow too long or to the point of becoming toxic.

Grief suppressed can take root and produce negative fruit such as anger, regret, bitterness, rejection, abandonment, loneliness and depression. These fruit are not the good fruit (characteristics) produced by the Spirit of God as outlined in Galatians 5:22-23. Oftentimes, due to human nature, we tend to compartmentalize those areas over which we feel we have control. Although everything we go through should be given to Him to guide us, the reality is that is not the case. When we choose to retain that which only God can heal, we place ourselves in a position to be controlled by the enemy, like a puppet on a string. The Lord tells us in Psalm 55:22 to *"cast your burden on the Lord and He will take care of you. He will not permit the godly to slip and fall."* Some versions of the Bible say that He will not let you be shaken or moved. The beauty of God's Word is that it provides guidance and direction for everything that we are and will experience in life. No, life will not be easy. As Believers, we are told that we will have trouble but God also tells us that He's with us during these times. His Word also tells us to trample on the enemy for God has given us power and authority over him.

Within the last seven years, I have lost five very significant people in my life, along with the threat of losing my daughter and the pending dissolution of my marriage. During that period, I really didn't have much opportunity to grieve like most people because I was too busy trying to keep someone else from falling apart. For the most part, all those whom I was led to support recovered well, except one. But God used that "one" to show me what happens when you don't allow yourself to grieve. God, in His infinite wisdom, used a phased approach to allow me the opportunity to heal as time passed.

He first spoke to me about legacy. With legacy, He showed me what my loved ones taught me throughout their lives. What are the key takeaways to remember them positively? For even in adverse situations, good can result. All things truly do work together for the good.

The greatest legacy left behind was Jesus. I was taught the things and ways of God so that I'd be willing to accept Him as my Lord and Savior and also willing to be in relationship with Him for He loved me and cared for me like no other. It was an opportunity to see the beauty and blessing in the gift of this legacy so that my children could learn them as well and pass them on to future generations. Also, it's a gift that could be shared with others regardless of their position in my life.

Secondly, I was taught gratitude. We need to learn to be grateful in all things including the

situations we go through. For through this gratitude, we will grow in love, in strength, in joy, in
peace, in patience, in understanding, in wisdom,
in revelation knowledge, in peace, in long-suf-
fering, in meekness, in kindness, in goodness and
in faith.

Gratitude will teach us to appreciate what we
do have, even if it's not what we want. Gratitude
teaches us that we have what we need to do what
is required for that particular day. Each day that
we are given by God is another opportunity to
experience the beauty of all that God has given
us through our gifts and loved ones. Each day is
another opportunity to be a better "me" than the
day before. Sun Gazing.com posted a message on
Facebook that I really could connect with. It stated,
"I am in competition with no one. I have no desire
to play the game of being better than anyone. I am
simply trying to be better than the person I was
yesterday." When you have the spirit of gratitude,
you are simply grateful for who God created you
to be. His validation is enough.

Thirdly, I learned how to live and to love life.
Each day, God grants us another opportunity to
serve Him, to get "it" right (whatever your "it"

may be), to serve His people and to experience things that we may never have experienced or may never have the opportunity to experience again. Each day is a chance to bless Him and praise Him all the more. It's a new day to celebrate Him and share His Word and His goodness with all those whom we encounter. God does not intend for us to have a "woe is me" mentality. John 10:10 in the Bible, teaches us that *"He came so that we may have life and have it more abundantly."*

Fourth, I learned how to better love and appreciate those with whom God has connected me. Granted, there were those in my life who may not have had the best intentions, for some had motives and their own agenda. However, God is teaching me agape love and compassion. He's showing me how to walk in grace and mercy. The paraphrase from Jesus' Sermon on the Mount (Matthew 7:12) *"do unto others as you would have them do unto you"* has become very real to me. In other words, treat others the way you want to be treated. For example, if someone gave you a lot of excuses, broken promises, lied, cheated, etc., how would that make you feel? So, why on earth would you choose to do that to someone else? By doing so, you are essentially saying this is how I want to be treated.

The fifth and last point I'd like to share is that there are times that God may take someone prematurely because He was sparing them and their loved ones' additional pain, suffering and agony. We must remember the death of our loved ones is not about us at all. It's about God's purpose in their lives being fulfilled. We don't know the mind of God in its infinite wisdom. But, we <u>do</u> know that He will reveal to us those things that we need to know and that He will never leave us nor forsake us. As a matter of fact, Deuteronomy 29:29 (KJV) teaches us that *"The secret things belong unto the Lord our God: but those things which are revealed belong unto us and to our children forever, that we may do all the words of this law."* In our grieving times, we must take the focus off ourselves, seek God for understanding in what we are to receive from the grievous situation we are experiencing and then trust that He knows best. The road may not be easy but the end result is certainly rewarding.

REFLECTIONS

_____

_____

_____

_____

_____

_____

_____

_____

_____

_____

_____

_____

_____

_____

_____

_____

Chapter 6

TEARS OF PERSECUTION

"God blesses those who are persecuted for doing right, for the Kingdom of Heaven is theirs God blesses you when people mock you and persecute you and lie about you and say all sorts of evil things against you because you are my followers. Be happy about it! Be very glad! For a great reward awaits you in heaven. And, remember, the ancient prophets were persecuted in the same way." Matthew 5: 10-12 NLT

PERSECUTION IS DEFINED as "hostility and ill-treatment, especially because of race or political or religious belief." It is "persistant annoyance or harassment." It's "a campaign to exterminate, drive away or subjugate a person because of their membership in a group or their beliefs" (Google[8] and Dictionary.com[9]).

Persecution today is running rampant. We see it everywhere. People are persecuted in their homes, on their jobs, in their churches and even in public venues such as malls, airports, train stations, etc. Sadly, people are also persecuted because their views do not line up with the person in control. What's even worse, the one that is being persecuted isn't being arrogant, unruly, vindictive or manipulative. They simply have taken a stance and stated they are not in agreement with the person who is in a leadership position – their superior, if you will. And, what's worse is the fact that this stand is taken against them when they were *asked* their opinion/view of a particular matter. There's an old saying that goes like this, "if you don't want to know, then don't ask me." Yet, when asked, people say vehemently that they want to hear the truth; however and in reality, they generally cannot handle it, particularly when it is based on God's Word. I often wondered, "Then why ask?" because it's clear the person didn't want to know or accept what you had to say. Persecution, to me, is a form of bullying. It usually manifests itself, particularly in the workplace, as dismissiveness, getting overlooked for promotions or simply ignoring a person's presence. What's hurtful is when persecution comes from a leader who is secretly or subconsciously intimidated by the confidence exuded by their staff member. Instead of tapping into the gifts and talents of their staff member to make the organization a better place, they mistreat and misuse the gift that has been given to them.

The most grievous of all is when the persecutor claims to be a Believer in Christ, as well as a Minister of the Gospel and/or a Prophet or Prophetess and their staff member is a Christian, simply walking in the ways of God. This type of persecution is extremely painful for the staff member, who is working under this type of leader but still trying to display the characteristics of Christ. While this is happening, the leader is exhibiting all the characteristics of satan and sadly, Christ cannot be seen in their actions or walk at all. Not only is it hurtful; it's a mockery to the testament of who God is and all for which He stands. Your heart and your spirit are telling you one thing; yet, your mind cannot fathom that this person is acting the way they do, broadcasting at the same time that they are a "child of the Most High God", quoting scriptures and asking at random times to pray with and for you.

I worked in such an environment for many years. As I grew stronger in the Lord, the persecution began to increase. Every time the enemy would set a trap or find fault in my work, God would protect, provide and prevail. There were times when I thought it was just me, but soon learned I was not the only one. The environment was toxic and the management team (or a majority of them shall I say) were the prime persecutors. If you didn't constantly tell them how great and wonderful they were, agreed with their lies, weren't willing to be manipulative, deceptive and disingenuous, you were an outcast. There was no such thing as fighting for yourself or the staff who reported to you. Selfishness, elitism, racism, classism and sexism were the rules of the game. Integrity was a thing of the past. So, I'm sure you can imagine that standing up for righteousness was like signing your death warrant. But for Christ I live and for Christ I die!

It's funny...I used to run into former co-workers and they always looked 10-20 years younger. I realized it was because they no longer were walking in a toxic cesspool. They may have been cast down for a minute, but they always rose to higher heights. Especially, those former co-workers who had a geniune love for the Lord.

In every organization, there is someone who would like to be known as the "Queen Bee". Our organization was no different. We had the Queen Bee, with the longstanding tenure and then the "New Queen", who was vying for the throne. It was never quite clear in the end who was actually leading the pack for both of them had their own way of charming the head of the organization. But with the longstanding Queen, she was clearly disturbed if someone looked better, dressed better, drove a better car, lived in a better house, was well-educated, intelligent and personable. Such a person was automatically deemed a target. Queen Bee was very strategic and manipulative. She often strategized a person's demise and/or manipulated a situation in an attempt to force the person to leave. She was the kind of person a former boss used to say could make chicken poop seem like chicken salad!

I would often hear people say that they could not wait until the day came when she "got hers". I must admit, while I was there, there were times when I felt that way too. I cried many a silent tear behind her actions concerning me as it related to blocking promotions and raises, manipulating the organization's healthcare package so that management couldn't see that she poorly managed large-scale cases, and the vile rumors she spread concerning employees for which she wanted to create the perception of persona no grata.

She wasn't the only one. "higher-ups" in the organization were just as bad. They used some to get rid of others for personal gain and were experts at being hypocritical. The things that were hidden from executive management would make one cringe. I'm sure if those individuals were aware of all the shenanigans and how disrespectfully they were being spoken of, they would have fired the majority of those persons. They also would have realized that the organization had lost a lot of strong, dedicated and committed employees due to personal insecurites and personality conflicts within their own management team. Funny thing is, if the higher-ups of the organization trusted more in the inborn intelligence they possessed, as opposed to the lies and inuendos of the two Queens they had surrounding them, the organization would have performed at a much higher level than it does today. The perception that employees left because they could not handle the direction in which the organization was moving was a pack of untruths covered up during management offsite meetings and discussed over a resort infused eight-course meal.

Naturally, one can guess that there were many times, being the bold soldier I am, I wanted to tell them a "thing or two" and then walk straight out the door. However, the Lord spoke to me. Simply put, He had called me to a higher standard and His glory must be revealed. He showed me that I was dealing with a Jezebel spirit and unbeknownst to the one under its control, I knew all that was going on. Years of mental abuse began to manifest itself in physical pain. The more I worked, accomplished and achieved, the more I was persecuted. I began to suffer from migraines and back spasms for days, weeks and months on end. Finally, I took a vacation with some very dear sister-friends, with whom I travel every year and prayed, asking God for direction and healing. He simply kept saying, "I will not allow you to continue to cast your pearls before swine." Upon hearing His voice, Matthew 7:6 (NIV) became very real to me, "*Do not give dogs what is sacred; do not throw your pearls to pigs. If you do, they may trample them under their feet, and turn and tear you to pieces."* I was supposed to have submitted my resignation the year before, but factors such as a very good income, my daughter's health condition, and the underlying hope that they would do right, weighed heavily on my decision to stay. God simply said, "I gave you that income and provided for you in all things. Don't you know that I can replenish that and more?" What also came to mind was a statement made by a former employee who also left due to the toxicity of the environment. He simply said, "you can't continue to play around with snakes and not expect to get bit." So simply stated, yet so profoundly true. What I didn't realize at the time that I finally submitted my resignation is that I had been catapulted into my destiny. I was to start my own business and go into full-time ministry. I'm proud today to say that I'm in the midst of doing both and loving every minute of it. Yes, I have some challenges, but certainly not any to the magnitude of what I had before and certainly nothing that can't be overcome. My silent tears of agony turned into public tears of joy.

How many can guess that work wasn't the only place where I suffered persecution? I also suffered it at church. I believe persecution amongst the saints of God, whether at church, an outside ministry or an organization is the absolute worse. I must admit that it's very disconcerting to me because there is enough work to go around. The Bible tells us that *"the harvest is plentiful, but the laborers are few" (Matthew 9:37 ESV).* That means there is a lot of work to do, but not enough sincere workers. I believe each of us is given certain giftings to do certain things. The areas I excel in may not be the same for you and vice versa. But, just in case there is the distinct possibility that we both excel in the same area, doesn't mean we don't have our own specific field to tend. If we focus on what we are supposed to do, we will all have bumper crops of new followers in Christ. I also liken it to fishing. Jesus told Peter, "I will make you a fisher of men." Just like there are different types of fish in the ocean, there are different types of personalities of men. The bait that appeals to one fish may not appeal to the other. So it is with the delivery of the Word. My style of preaching may be different from yours. Craft your style as I will craft mine through the study of God's

Word, just as fisherman craft their understanding of which bait works best for certain types of fish. If we all put our best foot forward, working under the direction of the Holy Ghost, we will yield a good return of new Believers.

We are to walk in love because God is love and His Spirit dwells within us. If we are displaying characteristics of being rude, jealous, puffed up and envious, then we are not walking in love. And, if we are not walking in love, we are not glorifying God. No one person, aside from God, can capitalize on being gifted and perfect in all areas. And, if we cannot be excited for our brother and sister in Christ and the growth and movement of God in their lives, we need to check our love meter. Chances are, it's broken.

There was a time when I would get so discouraged to the point of cringe when I faced persecution in the church. But, as I got stronger in the Word of God, it was clear that because He was persecuted so shall I be, because He lives in me. What would make me think that I was better than Him and should be excused from suffering?

I also learned to pray for the persecutors, those who were insistent on causing division within the

Body of Christ. I had to pray in order not to yield to the flesh. For the Word says, *"…Vengeance is mine; I will repay, saith the Lord." (Romans 12:19 KJV)* He also said, *"Sit at my right hand until I make your enemies a footstool for your feet." (Psalm 110:1 NIV)* In other words, God was going to take care of those who rose up against me because it wasn't me that they were up against, it was the God in me. My desire is that no one gets left behind. With that said, the greatest weapon you have against your persecutors is to pray for them. In doing so, God will turn your tears into joy and He will also show you rewards you earned for persevering and moving at His direction. For me, it was freedom from bondage and a closer walk with the Lord. The closer walk has taken me to a higher level of love, faith and trust in Him. I'm more yielded to the things of God than I was a year or two ago. Whoever had issues with me then because of the level of anointing that was on my life needs to watch out! Here I come, for *"…greater is He that is in you than He that is in the world…"! (1 John 4:4 KJV)*

REFLECTIONS

Chapter 7

TEARS OF FINANCIAL MATTERS

*"Bring all the tithes into the storehouse so there
will be enough food in my Temple. If you do,
says the Lord of Heaven's Armies, I will open
up the windows of heaven for you. I will pour
out a blessing so great you won't have enough
room to take it in! Try it! Put me to the test!"
Malachi 3:10 (NLT)*

WILL A MAN rob God? We don't like to think
that this is true of us. Yet, we do rob God when
we don't bring our tithes and offerings into the
storehouse (the church). A tithe is one tenth of
the money you receive. Period. Back during Old
Testament times, it was what they yielded in those
things they could sell -- crops, products, animals,
etc. Today it's that green paper that we love so

so dearly called m-o-n-e-y. The Bible is clear that when we rob God, we come under a curse. The only way to remove the curse is to repent and turn from our wicked ways. When we do so, God heals our land (all that He has given us and all for which we are responsible). To heal the land is to restore it so that it will begin producing what it was intended or purposed to do.

For me, my tears in this area were due to my choices. Pure and simple, I did not always tithe. I always gave an offering but it was not always my full ten percent. I will admit that I got caught up in the many traps and snares of the enemy; some willingly and some unknowingly because I was not fully utilizing the gift of discernment God had given me. I had gone through a season of losing houses, cars and land (as my elders would say) but then "God got a hold of me". I had to learn how to respect money for the sole purpose for why we have it – to use it for the upbuilding of His Kingdom. Yes, God will bless you with your heart's desire, but your desire must not take precedent over His work!

I also had to learn the principle of "earmarking". God will earmark certain dollars for certain things.

We are to follow His instructions and use the money specifically for what it was intended. I had to learn that the concept on which I was raised of "robbing Peter to pay Paul" was not of God and no longer acceptable for where He was taking me. As a matter of fact, God said "What are you going to do now that Peter doesn't have it for you to rob?" A very hard lesson to learn but a lesson nonetheless. God was, in essence, telling me to trust Him and not what my limited mind told me to do. I recall one time when my best friend said to me, "God can do more with 90% than we could ever do with 100%." And, oh, how right she was!

When it came to tithing, I had to learn that you don't tithe off of what you have left <u>after</u> you pay all your bills but <u>before</u> you pay all your bills. Because if you wait until after, you will never be able to pay your whole tithe. Furthermore, God told me to stop viewing the tithe as a bill. It's <u>not</u> a bill. It's a tithe. A bill is something you <u>have to</u> pay due to a service rendered or a product purchased. A tithe is a tenth of what the Lord has blessed you with through some means of income, that will be used for kingdom business. It's something you <u>want to</u> do out of obedience to Him and His Word.

The tears came much stronger, not because I was in debt, but as a result of finding myself repeating a vicious cycle. I could not understand "Why?" because I felt I had learned the lesson. So, why was I going through this <u>again</u>? Then, the Lord spoke clearly through the teachings of Pastor Chuck Pierce[10] (paraphrase) and said that the journey through the valley this time was not due to disobedience but so that I could snatch back all that was lost and grab the hidden treasures that had been stolen from me. I was going to recover all! I had to see that even in the midst of my valley, God was there with me. All I had to do was understand that He was not going to leave me, forsake me, or let me fall. Not only am I walking in His authority, I'm walking with Authority Himself!

I've learned that the enemy wants and strives for us to be cast down; to feel like we are lacking. But, the Lord has told us in His Word (Psalm 23) that He is our Shepherd, therefore we shall not want (lack). We may not have the abundance that we want or are used to, but we certainly have what we need, and it's enough to sustain us.

The whole purpose of money is for the upkeep and building of God's kingdom. The amount of money we have is tied to our destiny and our purpose. It is to be used to fulfill the mission that God has called us to. The greater the purpose, the greater the destiny. To achieve the purpose that God has for your life, the strategically outlined steps (destiny) for you must be followed explicitly. God has got to <u>know</u> that He can trust you. Pastor Robert Morris[11] said it best, "If you can't handle your money, you can't handle your destiny."

My desire is that we all walk in the purpose and plans for which God created us and be all that He's called us to be. This desire is why I started a ministry with one of my best friends called Sisters With Purpose (SWP) Kingdom of Heaven Ministries, Inc. SWP's main objective is to bring understanding of who God is and how to develop and maintain a relationship with Him, while teaching others how "to walk out" God's Word, thus walking in purpose. Our goal is not to pull our sisters from their respective churches, but to assist in helping them go back to their church to fulfill the purpose for which God sent them there. We also strive to reach those who have been hurt by the church or who simply want to better understand how to apply God's Word to their lives.

We, as Believers, have got to truly understand that the riches we gain and the items we obtain are not to hoard, gloat on or brag about, saying, "I've got mine, now you get yours". The purpose is to care for the needs of God's children, being a community which thrives to lift each other up when down or going through, thus building His Kingdom in love. To be boastful is an invitation for God to snatch everything away and have you start over again. We are to be a blessing without waiting to be asked.

Here is my last point. By nature, I'm a giver. If I have it to give, I do, especially when I see a need. I sow into people, not so much because I'm expecting a return, but because I'm trying to help them get where God would have them to be. God has had to fine tune how I give in preparation for the season I'm walking into. It will take some adjusting but I'm open to His voice. My whole point in telling you this is that in all thy getting, get understanding. As outlined in Proverbs 4:7, it is the beginning of wisdom.

In this chapter, the focus was on money. However, God wants us to tithe not only our money, but also our time and talents/giftings.

We are not to be selective in how we do so but are to follow His instructions explicitly because our destiny is dependent on it. As a matter of fact, Bishop T.D. Jakes said something that would be most appropriate to share at this moment (and I paraphrase) "…our prayer requests should be for God to reveal and guide us in His mission for our lives, not for prosperity, power or position."[12] *"In all your ways acknowledge God Him and He shall direct thy paths (Proverbs 3:6 KJV).* When we follow the instructions of the Lord, focusing on completing the mission He's outlined for us (our assigment), all that is required and needed (resources) will come.

REFLECTIONS

_____

_____

_____

_____

_____

_____

_____

_____

_____

_____

_____

_____

_____

_____

_____

_____

_____

Chapter 8

TEARS OF JOY

"You keep track of all my sorrows. You have collected all my tears in your bottle. You have recorded each one in your book." Psalm 8, NLT

WHEN I LOOK back over my life and all that the Lord has done for me, my soul cries out "hallelujah!" I praise the Lord for saving me! There are so many things, still unspoken, that has transpired in my life that could have truly left me totally unhinged. I am a firm believer that if it had not been for the Lord on my side, I would truly have been lost and, as my elders used to say, "not knowing whether I'm coming or going."

I have witnessed physcial abuse of close family members, mental abuse and verbal abuse. I have seen the damage that can be done to a child who was raised without a father and ensuing self-esteem issues that arise as a result of the absence. I've even recently come to realize that I was looking for acceptance and approval in someone who isn't even happy with their own life. So, if they are miserable in their own life, how can I expect them to understand and appreciate what God is doing for me in my life and how He has kept me inspite of all that I've been through? I've learned and experienced the damage of generational curses and the importance of seeking the Lord for deliverance once the curse has been identified.

One of my greatest testimonies is overcoming and being delivered from the spirit of division that tried desperately to keep me and my sister apart. The spirit was emanating from one that I least expected. However, due to the events that have transpired over the last few years, the Lord knitted us back together and revealed exactly what we were dealing with. The restoration of our relationship has been one of my greatest joys and is certainly a testament to the power of prayer. The love of God truly does conquer all!

Through it all, I have learned how to trust and depend on the Lord. I can recall how my grandmother would always say that to me, during our one-on-one conversations. At that time, as I was young and/or going through my teenage years, I did not comprehend the fullness of what she was saying. However, the Lord has a way of recalling those principles of His that your elders instilled in you that you once may have dismissed. My recommendation to the younger generation today is to take heed to what your elders are saying. Don't dismiss everything as "they are old and don't know what they are talking about" or "times are different now and...". The truth of the matter is the players may have changed, but the game is still the same. Satan can only use your past as a constant reminder of your faults, mistakes and bad choices. However, he cannot do anything to waylay what God has planned for you and your future. As a young preacher of the Gospel stated, "My then is not my now nor is it what I'm going to be!" Hold on to the promises of Jeremiah 29! In the end, you will win for the battle of spiritual warfare is truly not ours but the Lord's. We just need to be armored for protection, which is putting on the whole armor of God (Ephesians 6), studying our Word to show ourselves approved unto the Lord, keeping our faith and trust in His promises to us, praising and worshipping Him in Spirit and in Truth! Those are the keys to ensuring a prosperous future in the Lord, regardless of what we see with our natural eyes.

My silent tears of sorrow becoming tears of joy was and is a continual process. When I feel myself being weighed down, I take the opportunity to sit down and reflect on how He has brought me through some very difficult and trying situations. In doing so, it really does solidify the saying that "if He did it before, He'll do it again"; but more importantly, when spending quiet time with the Lord, it's an opportunity for Him to heal you of all hurt. As you allow yourself to be healed, you will find that God will pull together the fragmented, broken pieces of your heart, creating a beautiful piece of Mosaic art. To us, it may seem fragmented and broken, but to God, our heart once "cleaned" becomes a thing of beauty. For, when we ask God to give us a clean heart, we are giving Him an open invitation to perform heart surgery and to fix all that was broken and/or disjointed. When He's done, although the process may be painful to revisit, the recovery will be rewarding. Once you are completely healed, you will learn how to guard your heart, allowing it to embrace only those things that will bring Him glory and joy! As a matter of fact, you will be taken to a place in your life where you petition God to align your heart with His so that your desires are His desires for you.

I would like to leave you with this thought, as you go through the journey of having silent tears of sorrow converted to tears of joy. Jesus came to set us captives free which means that any and everything that we can go through, have gone through or will go through has already been addressed in the Bible. The amazing thing is that God gives us a guide on how to live our lives and endure through His written Word, the Bible. As we peruse and/or hopscotch through its pages, we find that there is a remedy for every situation that we come up against. The key is the willingness to adhere to that which He shows us. We will find that even during our darkest moments, our valleys if you will, God is still with us (Psalm 23). As a matter of fact, He says that we will experience green pastures in the midst of our valleys. That's provision! Let's be clear, we may not always have what we want, but God will certainly make sure we have what we need! And, truthfully speaking, once you develop the ability to be content in all stages of your life, you will find that there will be an increase in those things that you want because you have learned to appreciate them, but more importantly, to share them with others for the upbuilding of His Kingdom!

"Surrender All" by Joni Lamb[13] was the tool God used for me to embark upon my journey of healing. I will never forget the life changing weekend when one of my sister friends brought me the book and one of my best friends kept my daughter for the weekend. For you see, at the time, I was a single mother and my son was away at college. That awe-inspiring weekend was time spent alone with God, to read the book and allow God to heal me of the broken fragments of my heart; fragments that were left in several places, ranging from events in my upbringing, hurt from past relationships and choices made. That weekend, the Lord intricately and meticulously knitted all the broken pieces back together.

As I remember Joni Lamb describing the process of surrendering, the result was the creation of a Mosaic piece of art called my heart. A piece of art that I've learned to cherish the most and guard with the utmost care. It was a process for which I will never forget. I'm eternally grateful to God for Joni Lamb being obedient to His voice and writing the book. I'm equally as grateful to Him for my two sister-friends hearing the voice of God and intervening on my behalf at the precise moment that they did.

I encourage anyone who is seriously ready and willing to be completely restored and healed by God to embrace a similar course. *Silent Tears* may have opened a door of reflection for you, but please don't stop there. Use it as your catalyst to heal from that which you have buried. Don't be angry with those who have hurt you in the past. For this book is not intended to glorify victims. Its intention is to reveal how God can heal the brokenhearted and restore you to the place where you can walk out His purpose for your life in Spirit and in Truth.

Psalm 8 tells us that He bottles up our tears! God pays attention to everything we are going through. He NEVER leaves us or forsakes us. If anything, it's "us" who does the leaving/running. Today, my desire is that you stop running from your pain and run towards the One who can deliver you from your pain. Allow God to turn your tears of sorrow into tears of joy and watch as He showers you with blessings, which starts and ends with His Love!

REFLECTIONS

_____

_____

_____

_____

_____

_____

_____

_____

_____

_____

_____

_____

_____

_____

PRAYER:

FATHER, THANK YOU *for the ability to complete the reading of this book. As there is the strong possibility that it caused the reader to reflect on their own life, let him/her seek You for guidance in dealing with that which has been revealed. God, please take him/her to Your storehouse and entangle Yourself within him/her. Restore us only you can, creating Your Mosaic masterpiece with their heart. And, Lord, once they have been healed, delivered and set free, let them share their journey with someone else, encouraging them to turn toward You and help them to also grow in their relationship with You. Lord, I praise and thank You for the opportunity to share what You have brought me through. If it has helped at least one person to achieve Your purpose, then my assignment has been completed. May You get the glory out of all that You put our hands to do. In Jesus name, Amen!*

"Faith and optimism can add years to your life. A bad attitude is like a flat tire; until you change it, you're not going anywhere." Denzel Washington

To God be the glory!

ABOUT THE AUTHOR

ADRENE M. WRIGHT, *affectionately known by her middle name, " Maria", is a native Washingtonian. She has been a servant in the body of Christ for over twenty-five years. Adrene was called to the ministry in 1992, while living in California, but ran from her calling for fourteen years. It was in 2006 that Adrene decided to stop running and "answer the phone". In 2007, she openly accepted the Call, under the Pastoral leadership of Pastor Lisa Littlejohn-Gillespie, Pastor of Hope Fellowship Christian Church. In 2010, Adrene and her family joined St. Judah Spiritual Baptist Church, in Washington, DC, under the Pastoral leadership of Rev. Linwood Grant. She currently serves on the Ministerial Staff and as the Chairperson for St. Judah's Women's Ministry. Adrene is known in the Washington Metropolitan Area through various speaking engagements and has been coined by a co-laborer in ministry as a "Woman of God who walks heavy with the Lord."*

In June of 2016, Adrene was led to leave her employer of over ten years and start her own business. Wright One Enterprises, LLC was birthed in July 2016, for the sole purpose of providing management consulting and administrative services to businesses, organizations and churches. Having been a scribe for most of her life, it was also in 2016 that Adrene was led to complete the assignment given by God and pen her first novel, Silent Tears.

Adrene serves as the co-organizer of Sisters With Purpose (SWP) Kingdom of Heaven Ministries, Inc. This ministry was re-birthed in 2008, having been originally established as "Ladies Night Out". Adrene, alongside her partner-in-ministry and dearest friend, Evangelist LaShaun O'Bryant, established SWP for the sole purpose of empowering women to become all that God has purposed them to be, walking in their destiny, while spreading the unadulterated Word of God. Since it's rebirth, SWP's outreach has extended to the masses, as the Word calls us to do. She currently serves on the Board of Directors for SWP.

Adrene is the proud mother of two children, DeMarco and Chelsea. Adrene currently posseses a Bachelors Degree in Business Administration from Lancaster Bible College, as well as certifications in the field of Supply Chain Management, Compliance, Insurance and Church Leadership.

Adrene is blessed to have the love and support of family members and friends. Her favorite scripture is Jeremiah 29:11, For I know the plans I have for you," declares the LORD, "plans to prosper you and not to harm you, plans to give you hope and a future."

ENDNOTES

1   Edward Mote, Lutheran Hymn "My Hope Is Built on Nothing Less", 1797-1874

2   The Learner's Dictionary, www.learners-dictionary.com, "choice".

3   Oxford Dictionary, www.oxforddictionary.com, "discipline".

4   Bishop T.D. Jakes *"Woman Thou Art Loosed"*, 1993

5   *Holy Bible Woman Thou Art Loosed Edition*, 1998 by Thomas Nelson, Inc. , Used by permission.

6   MegaFest 2004 Woman Thou Art Loosed 9 Disc CD Series, T. D. Jakes Ministries

7 *Holy Bible Woman Thou Art Loosed Edition,* 1998 by Thomas Nelson, Inc. , Used by permission.

8 www.Google.com "persecution"

9 www.dictionary.com "persecution"

10 Chuck Pierce. "February is the Key Month of Intercession! 28 Days to Develop a New Blessing Cycle!", www.elijahslist.com

11 Pastor Robert Morris, Gateway Church, "From Dream to Destiny, Fulfilling God's Purpose for Your Life, The Prosperity Test", 2011

12 Bishop Jakes, The Potter's Touch Broadcast on TBN, 3/14/17

13 Joni Lamb, *"Surrender All: Your Answer to Living with Peace, Power, and Purpose"*, 2008

CPSIA information can be obtained
at www.ICGtesting.com
Printed in the USA
LVOW07s0040120917
548366LV00001B/18/P